WID

NEW TECHNOLOGY

environmental technology

Andrew Solway

Evans

Published by Evans Brothers Limited

© 2008 Evans Brothers Ltd

Evans Brothers Limited
2A Portman Mansions
Chiltern Street
London W1U 6NR

First published 2008

British Library Cataloguing in
  Publication Data
Solway, Andrew
  Environmental technology. -
(New technology) 1. Green technology -
Juvenile literature 2. Pollution control
industry - Technological innovations -
Juvenile literature
I. Title
628.5

ISBN 978 0 2375 3426 4

Printed in China

Credits
Series Editor: Paul Humphrey
Editor: Gianna Williams
Designer: Keith Williams
Production: Jenny Mulvanny
Picture researchers: Rachel Tisdale
  and Laura Embriaco

Acknowledgements
Title page: Reuters/Corbis; p.6 Benjamin Lowy/Corbis; p.8 Paul Schraub/ www.calfeedesign.com; p.9 Ramin Talaie/Corbis; p.10 Matej Pribelsky/ istockphoto.com; p.11 Sanyo; p.12 Cree Lighting/NREL; p.13 Jim Sulley/Newscast; p.14: Concordia Language Villages; p.15 Lawrence Berkeley National Laboratory; p.16 ARUP; p.17 Ed Parker/EASI-Images/ CFW Images; p.18 SOM/Crystal CG; p.19 BioRegional; p.20 Rob Hill/ istockphoto.com; p.21 moodboard/Corbis p.22 James Holmes/ZEDCOR/Science Photo Library; p.23 Herbert Kehrer/Zefa/Corbis; p.24 www.iomguide.com; p.26 Solar Sailor Holdings Ltd; p.27 Marine Current Turbines Ltd; p.28 Peter Foerster/Epa/Corbis; p.30 CropEnergies AG; p.31 Hans-Juergen Wege/Epa/Corbis; p.32 Jim Jurica/ istockphoto.com; p.33 Neal Cavalier-Smith/EASI-Images/CFW Images; p.35 Peter Ginter/Science Faction/Getty Images; p.36 Reuters/Corbis; p.37 Walter Meayers Edwards/National Geographic/Getty Images; p.38 Scott Olson/Getty Images; p.39 Sarah Leen/National Geographic/Getty Images; p.40 Paulo Fridman/Corbis; p.41 Foster & Partners; p.42 Mark Ralston/AFP/Getty Images; p.43 Arctic-Images/Corbis.

This book was prepared for
Evans Brothers Ltd by Discovery Books Ltd.

contents

introduction

Today, the world is in danger. Scientists and leaders from most countries agree – if we don't do something soon, our planet will become unfit to live on. The biggest threat is global warming.

Can we save the world? The Earth is warming up, mainly because of the greenhouse gases that are released into the air whenever we burn fossil fuels (coal, oil or gas). We burn fossil fuels to get energy. Every time we turn on the heating, boil a kettle or drive a car, we are using energy, and most of this energy comes from fossil fuels.

At an oil refinery in Libya, waste gases are burned off as flares. Flaring burns as much gas each year as France and Germany use. This produces large amounts of carbon dioxide, so some refineries now remove waste gas in other ways.

CARBON DIOXIDE

Coal, oil and gas are made mostly from carbon. When they burn, the main gas that is produced is carbon dioxide. Each year, we release millions of tonnes of carbon dioxide into the atmosphere. This is the main cause of global warming.

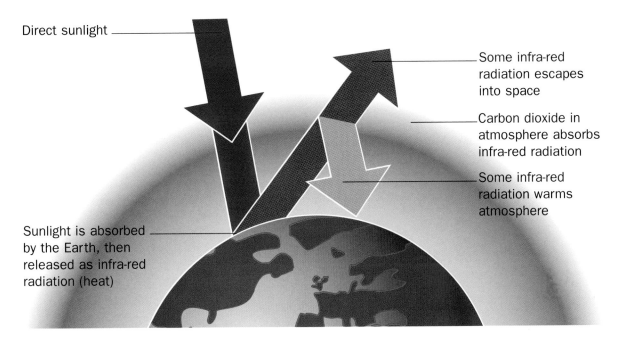

Direct sunlight

Some infra-red radiation escapes into space

Carbon dioxide in atmosphere absorbs infra-red radiation

Some infra-red radiation warms atmosphere

Sunlight is absorbed by the Earth, then released as infra-red radiation (heat)

Carbon dioxide creates global warming because it stops infra-red radiation from escaping into space.

To slow global warming, we need to reduce the amount of fossil fuels we use. How can we do this? Environmental technology can help.

How can technology help? Any kind of technology that helps to reduce our impact on the planet is called environmental technology. It can be as simple as a cooking fire that uses less fuel, or as complicated as a satellite in space collecting the Sun's energy. Environmental technology can work in several different ways. It can help us to use less energy, for instance by making more efficient machines and buildings.

Cutting pollution Global warming is not the only threat to our planet.

Pollution is another problem. It can affect people as well as other living things. Pollution can be caused by things that we throw away, waste products from factories, or even chemicals used by farmers. These substances can pollute the air, the land, rivers and streams, or even the sea.

Environmental technology can also help to reduce pollution. In some areas it has already helped, but we could reduce pollution much more if environmental technology were used more widely. Environmental technology can help us to find sources of energy that do not cause pollution or global warming. We can also use technology to help cut down on waste or to find uses for waste materials.

CHAPTER 1
saving energy

One way we can stop burning so much fossil fuel is to use less energy. People in developed countries use a lot of energy. They use energy to heat or cool their homes, for cars, computers, fridges, washing machines and many other things.

It also takes energy to make all the products we use. In contrast, countries in the developing world use much less energy. If every country in the world used energy at the same rate as the UK, we would need the resources of three planets to keep us going. If we all used energy at the same rate as the USA, we would need 30 planets.

We can save energy in very simple ways, for instance by turning the heating or the air conditioning down, or travelling by bike, bus or train instead of in a car. However, we can only make limited savings this way. Environmental technology can help us make other energy savings, by making the machines and other devices we use more efficient.

Saving energy can be as simple as riding a bike instead of going by car. If you go by bamboo bike, even better – it's biodegradable as well as carbon free.

More efficient cars Of all the machines that we use in our everyday lives, cars and other vehicles use the most energy. However, they are not very efficient. Only about 15 per cent of the energy in a car's fuel is used to move the car along or work the lights or the heating. The rest of the energy is lost, mostly as heat.

More than half the wasted energy is lost in the engine. Petrol and diesel engines work by burning a mix of fuel and air. They cannot work without producing heat, but this heat is wasted energy. Carefully controlling the fuel and air mix in the cylinders can make the engine more efficient. A turbocharger also helps to get more energy from an engine. A turbocharger uses a fan to push more air into the engine cylinders, and this increases the power of the engine. Many cars already have fuel control and turbochargers.

Hybrid vehicles, like this bus, run on two power sources – a traditional engine and an electric motor – in order to use less fuel.

Engines also waste quite a lot of fuel when they are idling, for instance when a vehicle is waiting at traffic lights. A new way to cut down these losses is to use an integrated starter generator, or ISG. This is a system that turns the engine off when a car stops, then automatically

WHAT'S NEXT?

Cars of the future could be powered by fuel cells and electric motors, instead of petrol or diesel engines. Fuel cells are like powerful batteries, but they make electricity using a fuel such as hydrogen gas or methanol, so they don't have to be recharged. Electric motors and fuel cells are far more efficient than normal car engines. Some fuel cell cars are being built now, but they are expensive. There is also the problem that hydrogen and methanol are usually made from fossil fuels. However, in the next 20 years or so we should be able to solve these problems.

Catch the Bus

GM HYBRID

starts it again as you press on the accelerator to pull away. The ISG also saves energy in another way. Most cars use brakes that rely on friction to slow the car down, and the braking process wastes energy. An ISG uses a different braking system that actually produces energy by generating electricity.

The best way to improve the efficiency of vehicles would be to change the way they are powered. An electric motor, for instance, uses energy much more efficiently than a normal car engine. It would also help reduce global warming if cars used non-fossil fuels. Both these ideas are discussed in Chapter 4.

Turning your TV off with the remote leaves it on standby, which means it takes electricity from the mains even while you are not using it.

Energy-efficient machines Walk round your house and count up how many devices there are that use electricity or some other kind of energy. The biggest energy users are heating and air conditioning. Other devices include lights, washing machines, cookers, fridges, vacuum cleaners, computers, TVs and radios.

STANDBY POWER

For electronic devices such as TVs and computers, the biggest waste of energy is when a device is on standby. It is using electricity even when it is switched off. Most devices on standby use only 10–15 watts of power (less than a quarter of the power of a light bulb), but there are many millions of them. In most countries, standby power uses between 5 and 10% of household electricity. In Australia and Japan it is even higher, at 12 to 13%. In the USA standby power costs about $4 billion each year, and produces 27 million tonnes of CO_2. In the UK, electronic equipment on standby produces a total of 3.1 million tonnes of CO_2, at a cost of over £500 million. If a million PC users unplugged their computers when they turned them off, it would save the equivalent of 250,000 litres of petrol.

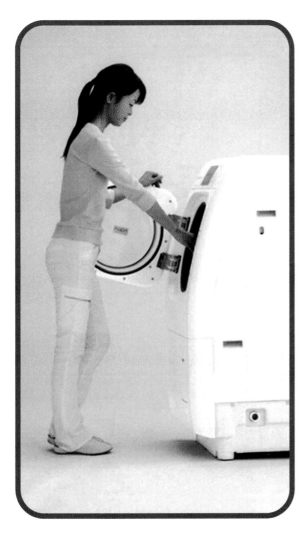

New 'air' washing machines like this one use ozone (an 'active' kind of oxygen) to clean clothes. Avoiding wetting and drying clothes when cleaning them saves a lot of energy.

WHAT'S NEXT?

As global warming increases, many more places in the world will have limited water supplies. Energy-saving washing machines and dishwashers are therefore designed to use less water as well as less energy. A new washing machine design from two Singapore students could make it possible to wash clothes without using water at all! The Air Wash washing machine uses negative ions and highly pressurised air to clean clothes without using any water. The designers are currently working on turning their design into a practical machine.

The biggest electricity users are in the kitchen. Washing machines, dryers and cookers use a lot of electricity, while fridges use less energy but have to remain switched on all the time. The best modern appliances use far less energy than in the past. Modern fridge-freezers, for instance, use less than a third of the energy of similar fridges built 30 years ago. New washing machines using a combination of steam and water spray for washing consume less energy, and the clothes are much drier at the end of the washing cycle, which saves energy if the clothes are then dried in a drier. However there are a lot more of these machines in use now than 30 years ago.

Smart buildings We are often told to turn off lights, or use less heating to save energy. However, it's easy to forget to do these things. What if it could all happen automatically?

Most buildings have some kind of automatic control over the heating and air-conditioning. For instance, your house probably has a timer system for hot water and central heating. Some offices and other large buildings have building management systems. These are computer systems that control the hot water, heating, air conditioning and sometimes the lights and ventilation too.

Most building management systems are not very flexible. They might be set up to keep all the offices in a building, or a section of a building, at a particular temperature during the day, or at the times when people are working there. However, a few buildings have better systems that are more flexible. For instance, the system in a hotel can be given the timetable of room bookings, and it will then make sure that each room is at the right temperature when people want to use it. A good building management system can save up to 30 per cent of the energy costs for a building.

More light, less heat LEDs (light-emitting diodes) are lights made using semiconductors (the materials used in microchips). LEDs glow at much lower

Low-energy fluorescent light bulbs are already replacing conventional ones. By 2010, LED lights like this could be replacing fluorescent lights.

WHAT'S NEXT?

Within 10 years, new homes could be fitted with 'intelligent' building management systems. The system would control the heating, air conditioning and ventilation so that rooms in use are kept at a particular temperature. It would also be flexible enough to allow people to open windows or turn on heating if they are too warm or too cold. Sensors would detect when someone goes into a room, and turn on the lights if needed and perhaps turn up the heating. The system could use weather forecast information to plan ahead, for instance by turning on the heat earlier on mornings when cold weather is forecast.

temperatures than ordinary light bulbs. This means they are more efficient and use less power than light bulbs. They also last a long time. Improvements in LED lighting have already led to LED torches and car lights. By 2010 we will have LEDs that are as powerful and efficient as the best kinds of light bulb. They will be used for house lighting,

This eye-catching lighting display in Jacksonville, Florida, USA, is an impressive advertisement for LED lighting.

street lights and many other applications. As well as being more efficient, they use less energy when they are turned on and off. They are also very thin, and in future they may also be flexible.

CHAPTER 2
improving buildings

In the developed world, buildings account for over half the total amount of energy that we use. They also produce over half of all greenhouse gases that contribute to global warming. A large part of this energy is used to heat buildings when the weather is cold, or cool them when it is hot. However, with the right design and modern technology, it is quite possible to cut the energy costs of a house or other building to practically nothing.

Planning for low-energy Making a low-energy building needs planning and design. A lot depends on what the climate is like. In a hot climate, the design needs to focus on keeping the building cool. This usually means small windows and thick, insulating walls on the side that gets the most Sun, and a good air circulation system to draw out hot air and draw in cooler air. In a cold climate the focus is on keeping the building warm. The side of the building that gets most Sun should have a conservatory or large windows to make the most of the sunlight, and there should be good insulation to stop heat escaping. Methods of heating and cooling that make use of the natural climate in this way are known as passive design. Over 6,000 passive houses have been built in Germany and the Netherlands. In 2006 a German language centre called the Waldsee BioHaus was built in Minneapolis,

USA, using passive design ideas. The BioHaus uses 85 per cent less energy than an ordinary building.

Planning the landscape can also be part of passive design. Trees and other plants improve air quality. Deciduous trees can provide shade in summer but then allow the Sun to warm the

This BioHaus low-energy building in Minnesota, USA, is one of the most energy-efficient buildings in the country. It uses 85 per cent less energy than most similar US buildings.

building in winter. When the CK Choi building in British Columbia, Canada was built, existing trees on the site were saved, and many ginkgo trees were planted. Trees like ginkgoes are especially good at cleaning the air of pollutants.

E-glass If a building has good insulation, this saves a lot of energy. The building will need very little energy to keep it cool in summer and warm in winter. The parts of a building that are worst insulated are the windows, because ordinary glass is not a good insulator. Low-energy buildings use new kinds of glass known as low-E glass. The glass has special coatings that reflect heat back from the surface instead of letting it through. Low-E glass can be combined with double or even triple glazing, with special gases such as argon between the layers of glass. Windows made this way are five times better at insulating than ordinary double glazing.

Some low-energy houses use windows in other ways. They are used as part of a smart building management system. Computers control the way that windows open and close, and

These windows at a research laboratory in the USA are photochromic. This means that when the Sun is bright, the windows darken to stop the inside of the building from heating up too much.

WHAT'S NEXT?

It may take 20 years, but two new kinds of material could revolutionise windows in the future. Transparent insulating materials (TIMs) are as clear as glass, but they do not let through heat or cold. They are made from honeycombs or plastic 'aerogels' (materials with billions of tiny air bubbles trapped inside).

Electrochromic windows have a coating that darkens when electricity passes through it. Electrochromic windows controlled by a computer could change automatically to cut down sunlight in hot weather and let it in when it is cold.

shutters cover the windows at certain times. These controls are part of a system that keeps the building at a comfortable temperature.

Changing the air If a building is draughty, no amount of insulation will keep it warm in winter and cool in summer. However, if a building is completely sealed, the air becomes stuffy and unpleasant. So in a low-energy building, the ventilation has to be carefully controlled. One way of doing this is to use heat exchangers. These are machines that swap heat between air coming into a building and air flowing out. If it is cold outside, the heat exchanger uses heat from air as it leaves the building to warm up cold air coming in.

The Eastgate office block in Harare, Zimbabwe, cools itself without air-conditioning. During the day, the building absorbs the Sun's heat, keeping the inside cool. At night ventilation cools the building down again.

HOW IT WORKS

The Eastgate in Harare, Zimbabwe is an office block which uses a special ventilation system to naturally cool the building. Some of the ideas for the building came from studies of termite mounds. Some kinds of termites live in large colonies in tall mounds. The inside of the mound stays at a constant temperature, even though it is hot by day and cold at night.

The Eastgate designers learned from the termites. During the day when it is hot, the thick walls of the building help keep out the heat. As air inside the building warms up, it rises and is let out through special chimneys on the roof. Cooler air is drawn in at ground level. In the cool of the night, the warm walls of the building give out their heat, and it is drawn out through the roof chimneys by fans.

Another way to help keep a building cool and ventilated in warm climates is to have an air space underground. Underground, the temperature is little affected by the temperature at the surface. It is cooler in summer and warmer in winter. If air from a building is circulated through an underground space, the air will be warmed in winter and cooled in summer.

Extra energy Even the best low-energy buildings need some energy, for things like heating water and running the electric lights. This energy often comes from solar power.

There are two kinds of solar power. Solar thermal power uses the heat of the Sun to warm up water. This is ideal for heating the water supply. Photovoltaic power is converting sunlight into electricity. Photovoltaic panels are quite expensive, and they do not produce that much power. However, an array of 20-40 panels can supply enough electricity for a house. Today it is possible to get photovoltaic roof tiles, wall panels and even 'glass' that can turn sunlight into electricity.

Mud, straw and newspaper Some materials need more energy to make them than others. An aluminium pan, for instance, has to be made from its raw material (bauxite), a process that uses huge amounts of electricity. More energy is needed to transport the aluminium to a saucepan factory, and to turn the aluminium into a pan. The total amount of energy involved in producing an object or a material is called its embodied energy.

Solar panels on the roof produce most of the energy for this sheltered housing in Surrey, UK.

WHAT'S NEXT?

The Pearl River Tower is a zero-energy skyscraper being built in the city of Dongtan in China (it will be finished in 2010). The designers plan to take advantage of the height of the tower to generate electricity. At two levels, there will be openings right through the building. The openings are shaped to draw in air, which rushes through a bank of wind turbines. Because they are in special 'wind tunnels', the turbines will generate 15 times more energy than if they were free-standing.

Using building materials with low embodied energy is a good way to save energy. You can build a house from low-energy materials such as mud, straw and old newspapers. Using recycled building materials, such as old bricks or wooden flooring, uses 95 per cent less energy than making new ones.

Rammed earth construction (see panel) is basically making walls out of

HOW IT WORKS

Rammed earth construction is a modern take on an ancient method. Earth taken from a building site is moistened with water to make a thick mud. This is then mixed with a small amount of cement. The mixture is then rammed into wooden moulds or forms. Once the walls are finished and dry, they are strong and weatherproof, but much lower energy than concrete walls. Rammed earth construction is used for houses in many warm climates, including southern USA, Australia and New Zealand.

Pearl River Tower is a 'green' skyscraper currently being built in Dongtan, China. This artist's drawing shows the two levels where air will blow right through the skyscraper to generate wind power.

mud. Mud, or adobe, has been used in this way for many years. However, new techniques mean that the material is far more weatherproof and long-lasting. Another new low-energy material is a kind of concrete made from lime and hemp. The material is as strong as concrete, but has the advantage that it allows water vapour to escape. This helps to prevent damp. Low-energy material can also be used for insulation or for floor and wall coverings. One new kind of low-energy insulating material is made from waste newspaper. The material is injected into cavities in walls or into roof spaces by a special machine, which blows air into it and 'fluffs it up'. The trapped air makes it an excellent insulator, as long as it is kept dry.

How much energy can we save?

Architects who design low-energy buildings combine many different methods of reducing energy use. Because they often use natural materials and make use of sunlight and natural ventilation, low-energy buildings are usually pleasant places to live or work.

Even limited design changes can make major energy savings. A purpose-built low-energy home, using passive design, can cut energy use by about 85 per cent, compared with a typical modern house. With the addition of devices such as solar panels and wind turbines, a building can be zero-energy (it needs no electricity or heating). The Beddington Zero-Energy Development (BedZed) is a group of houses and flats in London, England that do not need outside energy for heating, lighting and power. The buildings are designed to make the most of the Sun's energy. They are super-insulated and get water heating and electricity from solar panels. Brightly-coloured chimneys are ventilators and heat exchangers. Warm, stale air going out of the chimneys heats up the cool air coming in.

Solar panels and colourful rotating chimneys on the roof of the Beddington Zero-Energy Development (BedZed) in London.

CHAPTER 3
too much waste

As well as using energy, the way that people live in developed countries produces a lot of waste. At home, we throw away waste food, the packaging from things we buy, old clothes, old shoes and even old TVs and furniture.

Offices throw away tonnes of paper, builders throw out all kinds of building waste. Factories may have waste materials such as metal or plastic scraps. They may also produce waste chemicals, some of which can be toxic.

The total amount of waste we produce is staggering. In a year, the European Union produces 518 kg of waste per person. The USA produces about 11 billion tonnes of waste annually:

Across Europe and the United States, the amount of waste dumped in landfill sites like this one is falling, thanks to public awareness about recycling and greater concern for the environment.

WHAT'S NEXT?

Researchers in Cambridge, UK, are investigating the possibility of making a machine that recycles waste paper on the spot in an office. A large proportion of paper thrown away in offices is waste photocopying or paper that is creased or torn. The machine would remove photocopying toner from the paper, add water, turn it into a thick paste, then make the paper paste into new sheets.

that's about seven refuse trucks of waste for every person in the country. Most of this waste material is dumped: it may either go into a landfill site, or it may be incinerated (burnt), or it might be dumped at sea.

To deal with waste in the best way, we need to reduce the amount of waste we produce, reuse as much of the waste that we cannot avoid producing, and recover materials or energy from what is left.

Less packaging Many things we buy are over-packaged. If we cut down on the packaging we use, we avoid huge amounts of waste.

Simpler packages that need less material mean less waste. Computer-controlled, precision manufacturing makes it possible to make packages that use far less material than in the past. In France, for example, new wine bottles use 80g less glass than in the past, saving 50,000 tonnes of glass annually.

WHAT'S NEXT?

One way to get rid of packaging is to eat it! New kinds of packaging are being developed that are edible. Some of these are tasteless coatings that protect food from spoiling and can be eaten along with the food. Others are edible wrappings, made from fruit or vegetable purée, which can add to the taste of the food.

Another way to cut down waste is to use recycled materials for packaging. Amber or blue glass jars look attractive and can be made using over 60 per cent recycled glass. Supermarkets are beginning to try out recycled paper and plastic for packaging fresh fruit and vegetables and some milk bottles are now being made from recycled plastic.

People in many countries have now become accustomed to recycling plastic bottles.

♻ recycle

Another possibility is to use packages that are biodegradable (they break down fairly quickly). Paper and cardboard are biodegradable; these materials can be included in compost. Most traditional plastics are almost indestructible, but recently biodegradable plastics have been developed, though sometimes this means that the plastic simply breaks up into smaller pieces of plastic. Some of these new plastics are made from plant materials. Over time, they break down and become part of the soil when they are buried in the ground.

Recovering waste If we do have to throw things away, we can often recover some of the materials by recycling. Many countries now recycle metals, paper and glass. This reduces the number of bottles, tins and newspapers going into landfill sites. However, recycling plastics is less successful. Some plastics can be recycled. PET plastic for example, which is used for plastic bottles, can now be recycled, and recycled PET bottles are already being used. Researchers are now working on finding ways to recycle plastics such as PVC, and items that contain a mixture of plastics.

WHAT'S NEXT?

The best plant plastics developed so far are called polylactides (PLAs). They are made from a simple chemical called lactic acid, which can be made by breaking down plant extracts with bacteria. Another kind of 'natural' plastic, PHA, is made directly as tiny granules in some kinds of bacteria.

In future, it may be possible to 'engineer' plants to produce plastics directly. For example, plants such as potatoes and cereals produce large amounts of starch as a food store. However, by adding bacterial genes, they could be made to produce PLA or other plastics instead. Scientists have already engineered corn plants that can make PLA. In future we may be able to 'grow' a whole range of plastics this way.

This plastic sheeting is produced from recycled waste plastic. It is widely used in construction work.

Waste paper ready for recycling outside a recycled paper plant.

Waste food (but not cooked food or meat) and garden waste can be recycled by composting it. Paper and cardboard can be included in compost, too. People have made compost in their gardens for many years. However, in many places local councils now collect kitchen and garden waste for composting on a large scale. New methods of 'hot composting' can produce good compost in a few weeks. The compost can be sold to gardeners to improve the soil in their gardens. Another way of dealing with kitchen waste that is being tested is by biodigestion. This is similar to composting, but the process is quicker and produces two products:

FOR AND AGAINST

For

- Recycling can cut down on the amount of waste we produce.
- Metals can be recycled again and again.
- Paper, cardboard and glass can be recycled easily.

Against

- Recycled paper and glass are of poorer quality than the original materials. They can only be recycled once or twice.
- Material sent for recycling is often not well sorted, and recycling centres throw it away.
- Recycling centres are sometimes far away from the places where the waste is collected, which means that a lot of energy is used transporting the waste.

biogas, which can be burned for energy, and a liquid residue that can be used as a fertiliser on farmland, if it has been carefully treated to get rid of harmful bacteria.

Building with waste New materials are being developed that are made from waste. One kind of material, made from a mixture of crushed glass, ash and bitumen (tar), could be used to replace blocks of concrete. Researchers are also finding uses for rubber from old tyres. Researchers in the UK have produced a material made from recycled tyres that can be used for roof tiles. Others in Australia have developed a new way of mixing recycled rubber with new rubber that produces much better quality rubber than in the past.

Energy from waste Even the waste left after reusing and recovering as much material as possible can be put to some use. One way to deal with it is incineration (burning it). This produces heat, which can be used for heating or to produce electricity. Incineration also reduces the waste to ash, which takes up far less space in landfills than other waste. Burning waste produces polluting gases, but

This incinerator on the Isle of Man burns waste to produce electricity. Unlike many incinerators, this one produces very clean energy. It releases only steam into the atmosphere.

WHAT'S NEXT?

Metals were the first materials to be recycled, and metal recycling is the most successful. Scrap metals are first chopped up into smaller pieces, and then different metals are separated, Ferrous metals (iron and steel) can be separated from non-ferrous ones using magnets. Other metals have different densities, and these differences can be used to sort them. Once the different kinds of metal have been separated, they can be reused. Often the recycled metal is mixed with newly produced metal.

A new kind of recycling technique that might be used in future is cold bonding. Researchers at the University of Cambridge in the UK have found that scraps of aluminium or other metals can be joined to make new material by pressing them together. Cold bonding uses far less energy than other types of recycling. We may start seeing cold bonded materials in the next five years.

modern incinerators remove these pollutants from the waste gas. Incinerating materials like plastics also produces carbon dioxide, which adds to the global warming problem.

A better way of getting energy from waste is by gasification. The waste is heated in a low-oxygen atmosphere, and produces a gas that can be used as a fuel. This way of dealing with waste is still in the research stage. Test gasifier plants have been built in Japan and Germany, and a plant designed to burn 9,000 tonnes of waste a year is being built in the UK.

Dealing with sewage Cleaning up the vast amounts of sewage that cities produce is as big a headache as getting rid of other waste. Removing sewage also uses large amounts of water. Some low-energy buildings have found

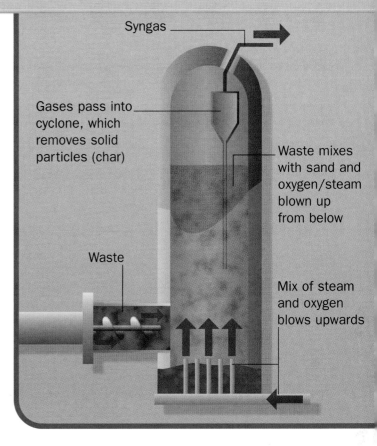

Syngas

Gases pass into cyclone, which removes solid particles (char)

Waste mixes with sand and oxygen/steam blown up from below

Waste

Mix of steam and oxygen blows upwards

There are several ways of gasifying waste. In this method (fluidised-bed gasification) the waste is heated by a mixture of high-temperature steam and oxygen, which is blown up through a bed of sand. It produces a gas called syngas, which is mostly hydrogen.

ways to deal with their own sewage. The CK Choi Building in Canada has composting toilets that reduce water use by about 1,000 litres per day. The compost produced is rich in nitrogen and makes an excellent fertiliser. Other dirty water is cleaned in special trenches containing reeds and other plants. These artificial reed beds make the water clean enough to swim in. The cleaned water is actually used for watering the gardens around the building.

WHAT'S NEXT?

Scientists have discovered that it is possible to use bacteria to generate electricity. This amazing discovery is very exciting because bacteria can live on all kinds of food, including waste material. In the future, it may be possible to generate electricity using bacteria fed on city rubbish or farm waste.

CHAPTER 4
new energy sources

No matter how well we conserve energy and reduce waste, we will still need large amounts of energy in the future. If we can get less of this energy from fossil fuels, this will help to cut down on pollution and global warming, and reduce damage to the environment.

One of the biggest areas of environmental technology is research into finding other energy sources that do not cause pollution and don't release large amounts of carbon dioxide into the atmosphere. To be useful, the energy needs to be cheap, practical and able to supply large amounts of energy.

Water power Hydroelectricity is electricity produced by harnessing the power of running water. Today, countries such as Norway and Paraguay get nearly all their electricity from

WHAT'S NEXT?

Scientists and car manufacturers are developing many new ways of powering cars. Hybrid cars, which use a combination of a normal engine and electric batteries, are already being produced. There are also a few cars that run on biofuel, and dual-fuel cars that can use either biofuel or ordinary fuel. Some buses and trains run on hydrogen gas. Hydrogen produces only water (steam) when it burns. At sea, new kinds of boat which are partly solar-powered or sail-powered can save a lot of fuel and cut down on carbon dioxide emissions.

The Solar Sailor is a ferry boat in Sydney Harbour, Australia. It is a hybrid boat, powered partly by solar panels and partly by a diesel engine.

hydropower. However, producing lots more hydroelectricity is not so simple. Some countries have no large, fast-flowing rivers suitable for hydroelectric power stations. Building dams for hydroelectric energy production can also damage river wildlife. In other countries, all the best hydropower sites are already being used.

One way we can get more energy from water is to use small power plants, or microhydro. These kinds of plants could be set up in many more places, to supply a small area or even just one house.

Tidal power is a way of getting power from the ocean rather than from rivers. A few tidal power stations have been built, but there are a limited number of places where the change in tide is large enough to produce large amounts of electricity. However, we may soon be able to get energy from the tides in another way, using tidal stream generators. These are underwater propellers that get energy from the movement of water in a similar way to windmills in the air. The world's first tidal stream generator is currently being built off the coast of Northern Ireland. The generator uses two huge, 16-metre propellers to generate electricity from the tide. A larger generator using five propellers is planned for the Bristol Channel, UK.

The first large-scale tidal stream generator is being built on the coast of Northern Ireland. This artist's drawing shows how the generator will look.

Solar power We have already seen that photovoltaic cells (solar cells) can be used to produce electricity for houses. However, at present they are not used for generating electricity on a large scale. There are several reasons for this. First, solar cells are not very efficient. Most only turn about 12 to 16 per cent of the light that falls on them into electricity. Second, solar cells only work during daylight hours, and they work best in strong sunlight. Third, solar cells are expensive to produce. However, some new kinds of solar cell promise to be much more efficient, and perhaps cheaper to make. These new cells have a coating of nanocrystals (a very pure layer of crystals just one molecule thick),

WHAT'S NEXT?

A small-scale source of power for the future could be solar-powered clothing! Flexible solar panels now being tested could eventually be made into sun-powered fabrics. You could recharge your phone or power your music player by putting it in your pocket.

which greatly improves the ability of the solar cell to collect energy. Solar cells made this way could be in use within five or 10 years.

Solar collectors, which concentrate the heat of the Sun, are another kind of

This solar power station in eastern Germany produces power for a small village. Banks of solar panels collect the Sun's energy and turn it to electricity.

solar power. A few small power stations use this kind of power to produce electricity. However, such power stations can only work during the day, and they are limited to warm areas.

Wind power Modern wind turbines can produce cheap electricity from the energy in moving air. In the near future, the amount of wind energy produced will increase, as offshore wind farms begin operating. These are groups of wind turbines built in places offshore where there are strong winds. However, wind farms can only replace a small amount of the energy produced by fossil-fuel power stations, and they only work well where the wind blows strongly for most of the year.

An idea for future wind power is to build 'flying windmills'. Scientists in San Diego, USA are developing flying wind generators designed to work in the high-speed winds of the jet stream, about 11 kilometres above the Earth. The first full-scale generator should be ready to test in about five years.

Nuclear power Nuclear power stations seem like an ideal alternative to fossil fuels. They are efficient, they produce no greenhouse gases, and they can make large amounts of electricity from small amounts of fuel. The technology of nuclear power stations has been tested around the world. However, nuclear power stations are very expensive to build, so they need to run for a long time

A prototype design for wind generators in the jet stream, high in the air. As the wind turbines spin, they work like helicopter blades to keep the generator flying, as well as producing electricity. The electricity from the wind turbines travels to earth down the tether (a wire connecting the turbines to the ground).

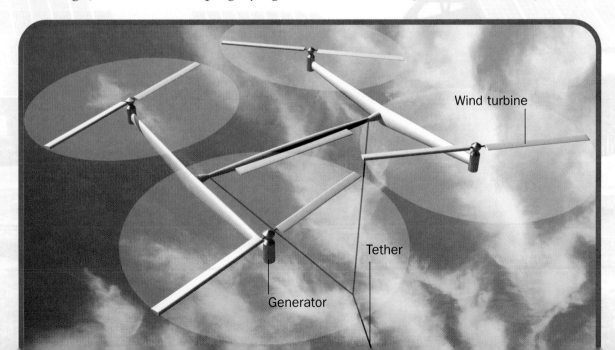

Wind turbine

Tether

Generator

to be worth building. Waste fuel from a nuclear power station is radioactive, and it stays dangerous for hundreds of years. No-one has yet found a good way to keep the fuel safe until it is no longer radioactive. There is also the risk of nuclear accidents, like the one at Chernobyl in Ukraine, in 1986. In the future, we may get energy from a different kind of nuclear power, called nuclear fusion.

HOW IT WORKS

The incredible amount of energy that the Sun produces comes from a process called nuclear fusion. Fusion is fuelled by hydrogen gas, which is turned into helium in the process. Scientists in many countries are working on developing nuclear fusion reactors to use on Earth. However, fusion reactors are extremely expensive to build, and as yet they do not produce much energy. One large research reactor in France uses magnetic fields to control the incredibly hot gases involved. Two other research projects, in the USA and in the UK, use lasers to compress (squash) and heat hydrogen to millions of degrees Celsius. However, none of the projects now under way is likely to produce any results until at least 2020. It could be 50 years or more before we have working fusion reactors.

Biofuels Biofuels are fuels similar to petrol, diesel or natural gas, but made from plants. When biofuels are burned, they release carbon dioxide. However, the carbon dioxide does not add to the total amount in the air, because the carbon has not been locked away in the ground for millions of years, as it has in fossil fuels. The plants absorbed the carbon dioxide from the air when they were growing. Burning biofuels only releases that carbon dioxide back into the air again.

A large-scale bioethanol factory in Germany. Each year, the factory turns 700,000 tonnes of grain into bioethanol fuel.

WHAT'S NEXT?

Scientists in the USA are experimenting with making biofuels from switchgrass. This tall grass grows very quickly and it will grow on soil that is too poor for food crops. Switchgrass can even restore nutrients to poor soil. It could therefore be grown in rotation with food crops.

Biogas made from waste material is not usually suitable as a fuel for cars. However, at a factory in Jameln, Germany, the biogas is refined (improved) to make car fuel.

Biofuels can be made from many kinds of plants, or even from waste materials. At present most biofuels are made from crops that could be used as food, such as sugar cane and corn. Making biofuels this way on a large scale could cause serious problems, because land that could be used to grow food would be used instead for fuel production. There is not enough good farmland on Earth to grow enough plants for both food and biofuels. However, other kinds of biofuel are being developed that are made from plants that grow fast and can tolerate poor soil. It is also possible to make biofuels from micro-organisms such as algae.

Biogas is a promising kind of biofuel because it can be made from waste materials rather than crops. The gas is made by breaking down animal dung and other kinds of waste material in closed containers called digesters. Bacteria and other microbes in the digester produce the gas. The process is similar to the way that yeasts produce the gases that make bread rise. Small-scale biogas plants are being used successfully in the countryside in India, Sri Lanka, Costa Rica and other developing countries. In Europe, cities such as Berne, Lille and Rome have large biogas plants producing fuel for buses. In Sweden there are over 1,500 biogas-powered vehicles, including a biogas train and 22 biogas filling stations.

CHAPTER 5
protecting the environment

Humans cause damage to the environment in many ways. We cut down forests, plough up grasslands and drain wetlands to make room for buildings, factories and farms. The gases released when we burn fossil fuels cause problems such as global warming and acid rain.

Oil refineries, chemical factories and other kinds of industry produce polluting wastes that get into the air and into water. The fertilisers and pesticides that farmers spray on their fields linger in the soil and wash into rivers and streams, causing more pollution.

Polluted water, like this untreated waste, is a problem in many parts of the world.

The damage to the environment does not just affect humans – it affects other living things too. According to the latest surveys, one in eight birds and nearly 70 per cent of all plants are now threatened with extinction. Most of

WHAT'S NEXT?

In the future, we may be able to reduce global warming using long, hollow pipes suspended in the ocean. The idea is currently being tested by a company in the USA. Wave motion moves the pipe up and down in the water. When they move downwards, colder water from below is forced up the pipe to the surface. A valve stops water going down the pipe the other way. Colder water from deeper in the ocean is richer in nutrients than water at the surface. This means that more algae and other plant-like creatures can grow in the water and these absorb more carbon dioxide from the air.

Tigers are among the most endangered large mammals in the world, despite efforts to protect them over many years. Conservation efforts mostly involve trying to restore polluted or damaged habitats, buying up land for nature reserves and developing 'wildlife corridors' which allow animals to move between areas of protected habitat.

these species are dying out because of the loss of their habitat. Many forests, wetlands and other natural habitats have been destroyed or damaged. Some animals, especially large predators such as tigers, survive only in small pockets, isolated from each other. How can environmental technology help solve these problems?

Living technology At many old mine and factory sites, the land is contaminated with substances such as arsenic and mercury, or even radioactive substances such as uranium. Cleaning up these

sites properly would be enormously expensive, so they are often abandoned. However, scientists are now finding new ways of cleaning up such sites with the help of living creatures. The process is known as bioremediation.

For example, in 2001 a team of scientists in Florida found that a common kind of fern, originally from China, could take up arsenic from the ground and concentrate it in its fronds. This fern has been used at contaminated sites to help get rid of arsenic.

Other kinds of bioremediation use bacteria and other microbes instead of ferns. In South Carolina, USA, scientists from the US Geological Survey used soil bacteria to remove pollution caused by a massive spillage of jet fuel that had happened some years earlier. Within a year, contamination had been reduced by 75 per cent.

WHAT'S NEXT?

Trees are good at cleaning carbon from the air, but one scientist thinks that an artificial tree could do the job better. Dr Klaus Lackner, based at Columbia University, USA, has invented synthetic trees that will filter carbon out of the air. An absorbent coating on its slats would capture carbon as the wind blows through them. Dr Lackner reckons that each tree would remove 90,000 tonnes of carbon dioxide every year, the equivalent of 15,000 cars. But will people be happy to see forests of artificial trees?

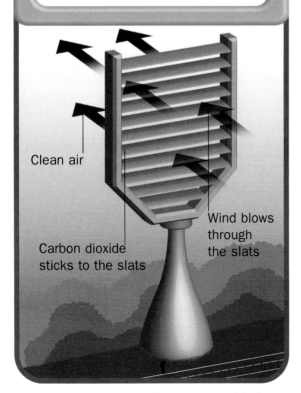

Clean air

Carbon dioxide sticks to the slats

Wind blows through the slats

How Dr Lackner's synthetic tree would clean the air of carbon dioxide.

Make our own microbes? When scientists discover a useful microbe, they look at its DNA (its genes) to try and find out more about it. In the future it may be possible to modify the DNA of microbes, for instance to make them better at cleaning up polluted water or soil. However, people have different opinions about genetically modifying (changing) microbes. Some groups or individuals think it is not safe to change a microbe's genes because we do not understand enough about the effect this will have. Others think that genetic modification could solve many problems.

FOR AND AGAINST

For
- Artificial microbes could combine the most useful parts of several different microbes found in nature.
- Microbes could be 'tailor-made' to clean up oil spills or clean polluted soil.
- They could help us learn more about DNA and genes.

Against
- We do not understand enough about the effects of changing a microbe's genes.
- An artificial microbe that causes disease could be made by accident.

WHAT'S NEXT?

In the future we could be cleaning up industrial waste with genetically engineered trees. Scientists in Tennessee, USA have discovered that they can add an animal gene to poplar trees which makes the poplar trees get rid of a poisonous chemical called TCE. TCE is a pollutant found at many industrial sites. It will take 10 to 15 years to fully develop this kind of bioremediation. In time scientists may also engineer other kinds of 'clean-up' plants. We will then be able to clean up industrial sites by planting a garden of these plants.

Scientists at the Bayer BioScience laboratory in Potsdam, Germany, use genetic modification techniques to improve crop plants.

Saving species

Saving the world's endangered species is an enormous task. All around the world, plant and animal habitats are constantly being destroyed by human activity, for instance clearing forest for farmland or for timber, or draining wetlands to build on.

To try and do the most good, scientists have identified 'hotspots' that have high biodiversity (many different animal and plant species). These biodiversity hotspots are where people are doing most work to save species.

Saving plants

Environmental technology is playing an important part in saving plant species in these hotspots. Often, researchers find only one or two plants of an endangered species, and there may be no flowers or seeds. In these cases they can grow new plants by a process called tissue

In a laboratory in Honduras, scientists are trying to save rare orchids by growing thousands of them using tissue culture. These orchids are the national flower of Honduras.

culture. Small pieces of plant material are grown in the laboratory, by giving them food and special substances called plant hormones, which encourage growth. With luck, the pieces will produce some shoots. Researchers separate these shoots, and grow them using hormones. The shoots grow into normal plants. In one hotspot in the Himalayas, scientists have saved some plants from extinction by growing them this way, then replanting them in their habitat.

Cloning Tissue culture does not work for animals, so other kinds of technology must be used. For endangered mammals and birds, cloning may be a way of producing new animals. Cloning is when the genetic code of one individual is injected into an unfertilised egg whose own genetic code has been removed. In the USA, a rare kind of wild sheep called a mouflon has been produced in this way. One method being experimented now is cross-species cloning, where one species gives birth to the young of an endangered species. Some very rare kinds of fish might be saved by a new technique being developed in Japan. The Japanese researchers took young salmon, and injected reproductive cells from an endangered fish species. The result was salmon that gave birth to fish of the endangered species.

Many people are opposed to cloning, and at present the technique is not good enough to be really useful in saving a whole species. However, some zoos are freezing small amounts of tissue from endangered animals, in the hope that in future it will be possible to clone new animals from the tissue.

Although these types of technology may help to save particular animals and plants, technology alone will not save species in the long run. To do this we need to conserve the habitats where the plants and animals live.

Mouflon sheep like these were the first endangered wild animals to be cloned. Some scientists think this may be a way to save endangered species. Others think it is a false hope.

FOR AND AGAINST

For
- Cloning can increase the number of individuals if a population becomes extremely small.
- If we collect and save tissue samples before animal populations get too small, cloning could provide an 'insurance policy' if a species almost disappears.
- Cloning may make it possible to bring back genetic material from animals that cannot breed.
- Any tool that might save endangered species is useful.

Against
- The science of cloning is still very untried. There are many problems with the process that still need solving.
- Many species have not yet been successfully cloned.
- Cloned individuals often have poor health and die earlier than normal.
- Cloning gives a false sense of security that populations of endangered animals can easily be revived.

Changing farming A lot of the food we eat is grown on large farms with fields full of one kind of crop, or in orchards and plantations containing only one kind of tree. Using this type of farming, we have managed to produce far more food from the land than we could in the past.

However, we are beginning to learn that this kind of farming has long-term problems. In some places it has destroyed the soil, leaving dusty desert areas. Modern farming methods can also cause pollution of the land and water. Farmers use fertilisers to improve the soil, and pesticides to kill off insects and other pests. Putting all these chemicals on the land year after year can cause long-term damage. Also, some of the chemicals are washed away by the rain and pollute streams and rivers. The polluted water can harm wildlife.

One technology that might help farmers to avoid fertilisers and pesticides is genetic modification. Genetically modified (GM) plants are plants that have had genes from another plant or animal added to them. Food crops can be genetically modified to resist pests or diseases, and so farmers do not need to use pesticides to protect them. However, many people do not see GM as environment-friendly technology.

One way of cutting down on the use of pesticides is to use genetically modified (GM) plants that can resist pests, like these cotton plants in the USA. However some people strongly oppose the use of GM crops.

Another technique is to combine modern farming methods with techniques used in the past. Co-planting involves planting together pairs of crops that complement each other. For instance, if wheat is planted with red clover, the red clover keeps down weeds and adds nitrogen back

FOR AND AGAINST

For
- Plants can be genetically modified to resist pests and diseases. Farmers then have to use fewer pesticides and herbicides.
- Some GM plants can produce better yields than ordinary crops.

Against
- Many GM crops are not sustainable: farmers cannot use seeds from crops they grow and plant them the following year.
- Some GM crops are designed to be resistant to pesticides. Farmers use more pesticides on these types of crops, not less.
- GM crops can cross-breed with ordinary crops and 'contaminate' them. This is a particular problem for organic crops, which are sold at high prices.
- GM plants could cross-breed with wild plants and create 'superweeds'.

to the soil. Scientists working in Canada have found that farmers can get good yields of crops using less herbicides and pesticides with techniques such as co-planting.

Acid rain Some of the chemicals released into the air by cars and factories contain sulphur or nitrogen. When it rains, some of these chemicals dissolve in the rain as it falls. They make the rain acid. The acid rain has its strongest effects on lakes and rivers, where it can be very harmful to fish and other water life.

The best way to stop acid rain is to stop releasing pollutants in smoke. Many new technologies have been developed to 'scrub' the smoke from coal power stations and other factories producing the gases that cause acid rain. Filters and devices that use static electricity get rid of most of the soot and other particles from the smoke. Materials such as powdered limestone, seawater and caustic soda are used in 'wet scrubbers' to absorb sulphur gases from the smoke. Improving the way fuels are burned, and recirculating gases through the furnace, are methods used to get rid of nitrogen gases.

Scientists test the acidity of a frozen lake in Canada as part of research into the effects of acid rain.

WHAT'S NEXT?

Scientists are investigating various ways of stopping too much carbon dioxide getting into the air by 'capturing' the carbon dioxide before it escapes from factory chimneys and car exhausts. Trapping the carbon dioxide in this way is relatively easy. Once it has been captured, the carbon dioxide has to be stored, to stop it getting back into the air. Some oil companies in Norway already store captured carbon dioxide by pumping it into old oil and gas fields under the North Sea. The carbon dioxide should remain buried in the rocks for millions of years.

CHAPTER 6
putting ideas together

Environmental technology is not just about saving energy, reusing waste, finding new kinds of fuel or improving the natural environment. It is about doing many of these things at once, as part of an overall plan for sustainable, low-energy living. If things are planned well, different technologies work together, and the results are better than when we use each kind of technology by itself.

One place where careful planning has made a whole city 'green' is in Curitiba in southern Brazil. Curitiba is famous around the world as an example of good environmental design. Each area of the city is designed as a unit, including houses, shops and businesses close to each other, so that many people can walk or cycle to work. For people who have to travel further there is a very efficient, fast bus service, with buses arriving every 30 seconds at the busiest times. Two-thirds of the city's rubbish is recycled. In the poorest areas, where refuse trucks cannot get to

the houses, people can take their rubbish to collection points and swap it for free travel tickets or food. The city has large numbers of green spaces, with thousands of trees planted by volunteers. Many public buildings are places that were recycled rather than newly built. For instance an old glue factory was turned into a theatre, and a warehouse became a community centre. These kinds of conversions kept down

Curitiba's buses load very quickly because tickets are bought in advance and passengers can get on through several doors. Even the design of the bus shelters helps.

WHAT'S NEXT?

A city in the United Arab Emirates is planned to be the first in the world to be zero-carbon. It will use no fossil fuel energy, all waste will be recycled and it will use 80% less water than a normal city. Masdar, as it is called, will be a research centre for sustainable development where nearly 50,000 people will live. The streets will be narrow and shaded, and no private cars will be allowed. No one will live more than 200 metres from a stopping place for an efficient electric personal transport system. A large solar power station will be built first: it will be ready by 2009. The power from this will be used for building the rest of the city.

An artist's impression of how Masdar will look. The narrow streets and covered walkways help keep the city streets cool in the hot climate.

the initial energy costs of the buildings. Despite having grown from a city of just 150,000 in the 1950s to 1.6 million people today, it is still a spacious, pleasant place to live.

Curitiba began to be built in the 1970s, well before other cities began to think about planning for a better environment. However, today other large cities are beginning to make their own sustainable plans. New York, for instance, has a 25-year plan, which will involve planting over a million trees, cleaning up pollution in the rivers and charging cars that want to go into the busiest parts of the city.

Planned from scratch One of the most exciting hopes for the future of the environment is the city of Dongtan, just outside Shanghai. Dongtan will be a city of 500,000 people, built on a swampy island in the mouth of the Yangtze River. Dongtan will have many lakes and canals, because it is built in a small area on one side of the island. Around the city will be parks, farmland and a large area of untouched wetland for birds. It is planned that the first stage of the city will be built by 2010.

HOW IT WORKS

Here are some ideas planned for Dongtan.

Cars and buses will run with hydrogen or other renewable fuels. Solar-powered water taxis will travel along canals and lakes. Cycle-paths and footpaths will make it easy to get around on foot or by bike. Most importantly, the city will be planned as a cluster of separate 'villages', so that everyone lives within walking distance of shops, schools and workplaces.

An energy supply centre will include a biofuel power station using rice hulls as fuel, wind turbines and a power station using waste material.

Low-energy buildings will be made using local materials, high insulation, solar panels and green roofs (roofs covered with earth and plants).

There will be two water networks, one for drinking water, one for toilet flushing and irrigating (watering) farmland. This second will be treated waste-water.

An architect discusses an artist's impression of what Dongtan will look like.

However, the new city will not just be a nice place to live: it will be a green city. At one edge there will be a large power station using biofuel made from rice hulls (the outside parts that are usually thrown away). Heat from the power station will be used to warm the city's houses and flats. There will also be a wind farm and a power station fuelled by the city's waste. As in Curitiba, the city is planned in small districts, so that people do not have to travel far to go to work or go shopping. The lake and canal system will not just be for show: it will also act as a reservoir for preventing floods. Buildings will naturally be low-energy, with solar panels to supply even more of the city's energy. All of the city's energy will come from renewable sources, and two-thirds of the city's waste will be re-used. If it works, Dongtan could be a blueprint for cities around the world.

Not the whole answer Saving the world from being damaged by global warming is a huge challenge for the human race. We have seen the many ways in which environmental technology can help – by saving energy, re-using waste, finding new kinds of energy and reducing pollution.

Technology alone will not save the world. People around the world will need to change their ideas of what is useful and valuable. When we buy a car, we need to value its energy efficiency

Iceland may be the first country in the world to switch over from fossil fuels to hydrogen. Many buses and some cars in Iceland already run on hydrogen.

more than how fast it goes. When we are looking for a new house, we need to check its insulation as well as the kitchen units. New technology will need to be coupled with new attitudes if we are hoping to save the Earth.

WHAT'S NEXT?

Iceland may be the first country to develop a hydrogen economy. The country has a plentiful supply of cheap electricity made by geothermal power (power from volcanic springs in the earth). This electricity is being used to make hydrogen from water. The first hydrogen filling station was opened in 2003, and a hydrogen-powered bus service began soon afterwards. Next will come hydrogen-powered cars, then fishing boats. By 2050 the whole country could be running on hydrogen.

glossary

algae Plant-like living things. Most algae are microscopic, but seaweeds are also algae.

bacteria Microscopic living organisms that multiply by dividing. Some bacteria cause diseases.

bioethanol A biofuel made up mainly of ethanol, a kind of alcohol that comes from fermenting corn or grain.

biofuel Fuel made from plants or from animal waste.

biogas Gas produced by microbes digesting (breaking down) plant or animal waste.

carbon The element in graphite and diamond, and the most important element in living things.

crop rotation Growing different crops each year, as a way of keeping the soil healthy.

deciduous (tree) A tree whose leaves fall in autumn.

DNA Short for deoxyribonucleic acid, a molecule that contains the genetic instructions for how a living being lives and grows.

embodied energy The total amount of energy needed to make a material.

fossil fuels Coal, oil and gas.

genes The way that living things pass on characteristics such as eye colour from parent to child. Genes are pieces of a substance called DNA that carries all hereditary information.

global warming The gradual warming of the Earth's climate.

greenhouse gas A gas that causes global warming if it is released into the atmosphere.

hemp A plant grown for its fibres, which are used for rope, cloth, and in some kinds of building materials.

landfill A way of disposing of rubbish by burying it.

methanol Also known as methyl alcohol: a colourless liquid that is used as a solvent, as a fuel and as antifreeze in engines.

passive design Design of a house so that it gets energy passively from the environment, for example from the sun.

photovoltaic cell (solar cell) A panel of semiconductor material that turns light energy into electricity.

sustainable Something that is sustainable can carry on indefinitely.

wind turbine A large propeller designed to turn in the wind.

further information

Books

Science in Focus: The Earth's Resources by Richard and Louise Spilsbury, Evans, 2006.

Sustainable Futures: Waste, Recycling and Reuse by Sally Morgan, Evans 2006.

Websites

EPA Student Center: An excellent site that has lots of information about all aspects of environment protection.
http://www.epa.gov/students/index.htm

Find out all about a real low-energy building. See how much energy the building uses each day, or what happens to the waste water.
http://www.oberlin.edu/ajlc/ajlcHome.html

Shell Eco-marathon: a race held every year to find the most energy-efficient car in the world.
http://www.shell.com/home/content/eco-marathon-en/welcome_global.html

World Solar Challenge: a race across Australia in solar cars, held every autumn.
http://www.wsc.org.au/

Green Progress: the latest news on environmental technology.
http://www.greenprogress.com/

Waste Online: all about waste and what we can do about it.
http://www.wasteonline.org.uk/

If you want facts on waste and recycling in the UK, this is the place to go.
http://www.defra.gov.uk/environment/statistics/waste/kf/index.htm

The Energy Saving Trust. If you want to learn about ways of saving energy, this is the place to go.
http://www.energysavingtrust.org.uk/

WRAP: learn about low-energy materials, composting, packaging and recycling projects.
http://www.wrap.org.uk/

Learn more about Masdar, the first zero-carbon city.
http://www.youtube.com/watch?v=ovly1dQ GKH4

Places to visit

The Eden Project,
Bodelva, Cornwall PL24 2SG, UK.
Eden is a living demonstration of green ideas in the biggest greenhouses in Europe.
www.edenproject.com/

Centre for Alternative Technology,
Machynlleth, Powys, SY20 9AZ, UK.
Since it began in 1973, CAT has been an international centre for developing environmental lifestyles. Visit their website at www.cat.org.uk/index.tmpl. The visitor centre is open all year round except early January.

Find an Eco-village near you.
Global EcoVillage Network is a network connecting places around the world where people are trying to live a low-energy, eco-friendly lifestyle. If you go to their website (gen.ecovillage.org/about/index.html) you can look up an eco-village near you. Many villages have tours and events you can go to.

Science Museum,
Exhibition Road, South Kensington,
London, SW7 2DD, UK.
Try out the interactive exhibition on energy, or learn about the weather and climate change.

index